More
Dedications
and
Readings
for Church Events

More Dedications and Readings for Church Events

Manfred Holck, Jr.,
Compiler

BAKER BOOK HOUSE
Grand Rapids, Michigan 49516

Contents

Why Another Book of Dedications and Readings?

There is never an end to the special events that congregations celebrate. In congregations excited about their witness, growth, and faith, there is a constant stream of occasions that demand exceptional recognition.

Pastors are always looking for thought-starters for preparing appropriate litanies, prayers, dedications, and readings for these special events. This book is an attempt to provide a vast resource of possibilities for ideas on developing a special service for these particular events.

In my previous books, *Dedication Services for Every Occasion* (Judson Press) and *Dedications and Readings for Church Events* (Baker) many services were listed. In this volume *More Dedications and Readings for Church Events* even more opportunities are set forth to help busy parish pastors meet this continuing need to set apart the special times in the life of the congregation.

Unlike those in the first two books, these litanies and readings are listed in alphabetical order in the Contents. This should make it easier to locate those services that may be helpful.

The readings and litanies in all three books have

8 Why Another Book of Dedications and Readings

been compiled from the "Handbook of Dedications"
section of the May/June annual planning issues of
The Clergy Journal magazine. They were all originally
submitted by parish pastors who had used them suc-
cessfully in their own congregations.

Manfred Holck, Jr.

Litany for Dedication of Acolyte Robes and Stoles

MINISTER: Inasmuch as our Lord said, "Let your light so shine before men" (Matt. 5:16), we light altar candles signifying that Christ is the light of the world.

PEOPLE: As our acolytes leave the altar they carry the light and pass it on, that we may let it shine in the world in the coming week.

MINISTER: That this might be done in beauty and dignity we come now to dedicate new acolyte robes and stoles,

PEOPLE: In loving memory of our departed friends.

MINISTER: In recognition of the lives and ministry of the following persons _____,

PEOPLE: We dedicate these robes and stoles.

MINISTER: To the blessing of many who will be uplifted through services of worship in which these robes are worn,

PEOPLE: We dedicate these robes and stoles.

MINISTER: To the glory of God whose love is expressed in and through our services of worship,

PEOPLE: We dedicate these robes and stoles.

MINISTER: Let us pray.

ALL: O God our Father, we come in the name of Jesus Christ your Son, who is the light of the world, to thank you for the lives of your departed servants. We thank you for their love and friendship, for their service to Christ and their friends. Grant that as we dedicate these robes and stoles we shall remember them with love and affection, and as these are worn by our acolytes, and as they light the candles, we shall recall that we are to be the light of the world. Challenge us each time we worship to leave your house and carry the light into the world, that others might follow it and come to you. In Jesus' name. Amen.

Trinity United Methodist Church
Shelbyville, Indiana
Richard D. Clark

Service of Recognition for Adoption of a Child

(Insert name of parents) have been the foster parents of _____ for (indicate length of time). By court order they have become the legal parents of _____ and desire that such action be recognized in its personal and religious significance.

We are happy to join with them in this service of religious sanction as a fitting consummation of this adoption, whereby they will be one family, in the sight of God, our common Father.

The words of Hannah concerning her son are the words of all true parents: "For this child I prayed; and the LORD has granted me my petition" (1 Sam. 1:27).

We have come today as a congregation to recognize and honor parenthood and to ask God's blessing upon this family. This is our privilege and responsibility.

It is recorded of Moses and Pharaoh's daughter that "he became her son" (Exod. 2:10).

It is stated that Mordecai adopted Esther as his own daughter (Est. 2:7, 15).

Paul refers to Timothy as his spiritual son, calling him "my own son" and "my dearly beloved son" (1 Tim. 1:2 and 2 Tim. 1:2).

As the marriage altar is the holy place of human love, so the home is the place of the nurturing of Christian values. Here is the guarantee of integrity and social purity. By the home alone can truth and righteousness be transmitted from one generation to another.

(Insert name of parents), you have brought _____ to the church for its blessing upon his/her adoption by you.

This then is a time of rejoicing, but it is also an occasion for the serious commitment to responsibility.

Do you promise to fulfill the duties and privileges of parenthood to the best of your ability and to look to God for the guidance of your family? (We do.)

Will you give _____ your love, protection, and guidance? (We will.)

Do you promise to instruct him/her in the Christian life and the services of the church? (We will.)

Do you affirm that you have given him/her your name and wish him/her to be known as _____? (We do.)

(Insert name of child), you were chosen to be the son/daughter of these two people whose hand you hold. They have promised to be your father and mother. Your name is now and shall be _____.

(Ask following questions if child is old enough to respond.)

Do you accept them as your parents?(I do.)

Do you promise always to try to be a good son/daughter and to make them happy and proud of you? (I do.)

Therefore, since in accordance with the laws of the State of (insert name of state), you have become the parents of _____, as a minister of a Christian church and as your pastor, I do now pronounce the blessing of the church upon you and your son/daughter.

(Prayer and benediction conclude the service)

Margate Community Baptist Church
Margate, New Jersey
Oran Presley, pastor

A Reading for the Dedication of Altar Candelabra

MINISTER: Without the light of your Holy Spirit, O God, mystery would vanish. Beauty would be unappreciated, people would worship themselves, and their hearts would soon fail them for very fear.

PEOPLE: Therefore, O God, to you for your holy, blessed inward light, we dedicate these candelabra.

MINISTER: Without the sun, the moon, and the stars and your priceless gifts to people, the world would soon be plunged into darkness. The strongest mountains would crumble, the tallest trees would fall, and all growing things would die.

PEOPLE: Therefore, O God, to you for the light of the sun, the moon, and the stars, we dedicate these candelabra.

MINISTER: Without Jesus Christ, service to others would be abandoned, love in human hearts would disappear, the scramble for things would injure the upward striving of the soul, and the visit of the shepherds, the gifts of the magi, and the song of the angels would be forgotten, and our hope would forever depart.

PEOPLE: Therefore, O God, to you through whom life and immortality came to light, we dedicate these candelabra.

Williamsburg Road Reformed Church
Bronx, New York
Millard M. Gifford, pastor

Litany for the Blessing of an Altar (Communion Table)

MINISTER: In the name of the Father, and of the Son, and of the Holy Spirit.

PEOPLE: Amen.

MINISTER: Our help is in the name of the Lord,

PEOPLE: Who made heaven and earth.

MINISTER: O Lord, open my lips,

PEOPLE: And my mouth shall show forth your praise.

MINISTER: Make haste, O God, to deliver me.

PEOPLE: Make haste to help me, O Lord.

MINISTER: Glory be to the Father, and to the Son, and to the Holy Spirit.

PEOPLE: As it was in the beginning, is now, and ever shall be, world without end. Amen.

MINISTER: O send out your light and your truth, let them lead me,

PEOPLE: Let them bring me into your holy hill, and to your tabernacles.

MINISTER: Then will I go unto the altar of God,

PEOPLE: Unto God my exceeding joy.

MINISTER: The sacrifices of God are a broken spirit,

PEOPLE: A broken and contrite heart, O God, you will not despise.

MINISTER: The Lord be with you,

PEOPLE: And with your spirit.

MINISTER: Lift up your hearts,

PEOPLE: We lift them up unto the Lord.

MINISTER: Let us give thanks unto the Lord our God,

PEOPLE: It is meet and right so to do.

MINISTER: It is truly meet, right, and salutary, that we should at all times and in all places give thanks unto you, O Lord, holy Father, almighty, everlasting God. On the tree of the cross you gave salvation to all people through Christ our Lord. We humbly beseech you, let your unspeakable loving-kindness and tender mercy be with us, O God. In your honor and for your glory we, your unworthy servants, invoking your holy name, do dedicate this altar (communion table). Graciously hearken unto our petitions and bless and hallow it; and grant that this our offering may be acceptable and pleasing unto you, who lives and reigns, one God, world without end.

Blessed and dedicated be this altar (communion table) to the honor and glory of God. In the name of the Father, and of the Son, and of the Holy Spirit. Amen.

"Blessing and honour and glory and power be unto him that sitteth upon the throne, and unto the Lamb for ever and ever" (Rev. 5:13b KJV) Alleluia. Amen.

First Presbyterian Church
Thompsonville, Connecticut

Reading for the Distribution of Ashes at Sea

We have gathered together at sea to return the ashes of _____ to the waters out of which life emerged.

The sea was the source of life in the beginning of our planet and water is the home of the unborn child.

It is fitting that these ashes be returned to the source from which all life emerged.

In the providence of God the death of the body from which no one can escape has come upon this, our friend and relative. We therefore commit the ashes of _____ to the sea from whence came all life and we commend the soul of _____ into the hands of God.

Distribution of the Ashes to the Sea

And now may the God of love within us and beyond us and in the earth and sky and sea, be with us on this day and forever. Amen.

Channing Memorial Church
Newport, Rhode Island
Philip M. Larson, pastor

Litany for the Dedication of Attendance Pads and Covers

MINISTER: We are happy to dedicate these attendance pads and covers to the glory of God.

PEOPLE: We dedicate them to the glory of God for use in our house of worship.

MINISTER: They help us know the people worshiping this morning,

PEOPLE: Praise God that people are important.

MINISTER: They help us know who first-time visitors are,

PEOPLE: Praise God, for we are glad for first-time visitors.

MINISTER: They identify new residents,

PEOPLE: Praise God, for we are happy for the new residents who are worshiping with us.

MINISTER: They make it easy for persons to let it be known that they may wish to join this church.

PEOPLE: Praise God, help our church to grow.

MINISTER: They can be helpful with address changes and phone numbers,

PEOPLE: Praise God that important information can be secured so easily.

MINISTER: They can help us to know who is worshiping in our pew,

PEOPLE: Praise God who helps us to know each other better.

ALL: Father, we thank you for all those persons who have provided these pads and covers for the evangelistic and friendship uses for which these items are intended. We ask the Holy Spirit to draw all persons into worship with us, be in Sunday school with us, that they may accept Jesus Christ as Lord and Savior. May all of us grow in our love and forgiveness of each other. We pray in the powerful name of Jesus. Amen.

The Onawa and Turin United Methodist Churches
Onawa, Iowa
Hugh S. Bird, pastor

Reading for the Dedication of Audiovisual Equipment

MINISTER: God brought light out of darkness,

PEOPLE: We thank God for light.

MINISTER: God created the heavens and the earth, and everything in them, giving life to the world,

PEOPLE: We thank God for life.

MINISTER: God revealed himself to mankind, saying, "I will be your God, and you shall be my people,"

PEOPLE: We thank God that we may call him our Father.

MINISTER: God sent his only-begotten Son to be the Savior of the world,

PEOPLE: We thank God for Jesus Christ our Lord.

MINISTER: God spoke to people of olden times and they heard and responded,

PEOPLE: We thank God for gifts of speech, hearing, and sight.

MINISTER: Christ died for us sinners, and established his church as a fellowship of those who accept his promises, and as a witness to the world,

PEOPLE: We thank God for the church.

MINISTER: God permitted people to learn the wonders of science and technology, the development of electrical power, artificial illumination, the transistor, metal-recording tape, and photographic equipment,

PEOPLE: We thank God for cameras and projectors and televisions and videocassette recorders and audio amplifiers.

MINISTER: God's world is so wonderful that we may explore faraway places and times, learning of our Christian heritage and mission to the world,

PEOPLE: We dedicate this audiovisual equipment.

MINISTER: In appreciation for the opportunities of inspiration, growth, and entertainment that many will enjoy from the use of this equipment,

PEOPLE: We dedicate this television, videocassette recorder, projector, recorder, amplifier, and phonograph.

MINISTER: In appreciation for all those who contribute time and talents and resources that the work of this church may continue and expand,

PEOPLE: We thank our God, the Father, Son, and
Holy Spirit. Amen.

Bethel Presbyterian Church
West Columbia, Texas
Leonard R. Swinney, pastor

Litany and Prayer for the Dedication of a Baptismal Font or Baptistry

MINISTER: It is our pleasure to accept and dedicate this baptismal font presented by friends and neighbors in loving memory of _____. On behalf of this congregation, I accept this memorial gift with our sincere appreciation and with the assurance that not only will it help to perpetuate the memory of _____, but it will also add beauty and dignity to our meeting house, and will become a place at which the most sacred vows are made. Please join me in the litany of dedication.

To the high and holy moment when parents bring their child to this place, offering to God the gratitude of their hearts and their vow to rear their child in the way of the abundant life,

PEOPLE: We accept and dedicate this gift.

MINISTER: And to the desire that every child brought here shall so grow as to always bless the day he or she was born,

PEOPLE: We accept and dedicate this gift.

MINISTER: And to the faith that sees in every child the hope of the world and the possible future greatness that is before us,

PEOPLE: We accept and dedicate this gift.

MINISTER: And to the remembrance that the holy man Simeon, when the baby Jesus was brought into the temple for dedication, prayed to God, "Lord, now let your servant depart in peace, for my eyes have seen the salvation which you have prepared before the face of all people, a light to lighten the Gentiles and the glory of your people Israel" (*see* Luke 2:29–32),

PEOPLE: We accept and dedicate this gift.

MINISTER: Baptism has long been an outward symbol of inward and spiritual grace, a moment of high resolve and direction of purpose, an act of which even Jesus himself felt constrained to partake as he began his ministry. It was of such significance to him, that in the Gospel tradition it is recorded that "Jesus, when he was baptized, went up straightway out of the water: and, lo, the heavens were opened unto him, and he saw the Spirit of God descending like a dove, and lighting upon him: And, lo, a voice from heaven, saying, 'This is my beloved Son in whom I am well pleased'" (Matt. 3:16–17 KJV),

PEOPLE: We accept and dedicate this gift.

MINISTER: To the acknowledgement of baptism as a symbol of cleansing and of the redirection of one's life, penitently seeking forgiveness for past wrongs,

PEOPLE: We accept and dedicate this gift.

MINISTER: To the intention to lead a new life, we have been baptized of water and of the Spirit of God, remembering Jesus' words to Nicodemus, "Verily, verily, I say to you, except a [person] be born again, [that person] cannot see the kingdom of God" (John 3:3),

PEOPLE: We accept and dedicate this gift.

MINISTER: To our own acceptance as a Christian fellowship of Jesus' final admonition to his disciples, "Go ye therefore, and teach all nations, baptizing them in the name of the Father, and of the Son, and of the Holy Spirit" (Matt. 28:19 KJV),

PEOPLE: We accept and dedicate this gift.

MINISTER: Almighty God, who has given and does restore to us those whom we delight in holding in memory, accept, we pray, the offering of this baptismal font, consecrating it by your power and blessing it to holy use,

PEOPLE: We accept and dedicate this gift.

MINISTER: And now, may all who worship here in these days and in the days to come, find inspiration therein, and be lifted up toward you, the source and summit of all beauty and life. We ask this in the spirit of Jesus Christ. Amen.

Granville Avenue Presbyterian Church
Chicago, Illinois

Dedication Prayer for a Baptismal Font

Gracious and loving God, we remember this day that you have given to us the opportunity for a renewed life through the sacrament of Holy Baptism.

Through the gift of your Son we know the meaning of life unto eternity. Through the gift of this baptismal font, we remember a life filled with love for you and dedication to your will. May each time that this font is used be a new occasion for renewed dedication to your will on the part of us who have already experienced baptism and a fresh beginning for those who will receive its blessing for the first time.

Help us to accept the blessedness of your Word and your way, so that in our living we may witness to the life of faith here remembered in _____. Our prayer is in Christ's holy name. Amen.

St. Peter's United Church of Christ
Amherst, Ohio
Joseph R. Foster, pastor

Reading for the Dedication of a Bible Stand

MINISTER: Blessed are those who keep his testimonies and who seek his Word with their whole heart.

PEOPLE: O, how we love your Word, O Lord. It is our meditation all the day.

MINISTER: God's holy Word is a lamp to our feet and a light to our path.

PEOPLE: Teach us, Lord, to study to show ourselves approved to you, workers who need not be ashamed, rightly dividing the Word of truth.

MINISTER: To the glory of God and Jesus Christ, the living Word.

PEOPLE: We dedicate this new Bible stand.

MINISTER: To the memory of the _____ family,

PEOPLE: We dedicate this new Bible stand.

MINISTER: We also dedicate this Bible stand as a symbol to show that we believe in the open, living Word of God.

PEOPLE: "All scripture is given by inspiration of God, and is profitable for doctrine, for reproof, for correction, for instruction in righteousness" (2 Tim. 3:16 KJV),

MINISTER: We also dedicate this Bible stand as a symbol of the means by which salvation in Christ comes.

PEOPLE: "These are written that you may believe that Jesus is the Christ, the Son of God, and that believing you may have life in his name" (John 20:31).

ALL: God's holy Word is "a lamp unto my feet and a light unto my path" (Ps. 119:105). Its words will I hide in my heart that I may not sin against God.

First Baptist Church
Ossining, New York
Robert S. Coats, pastor

Prayer and Litany of Dedication for Church Building Addition

MINISTER: Let us pray. Blessed be the space we have shaped for parking. Lord, you know the trials and tribulations of that effort. It is a joy to dedicate that space as a part of our mission of reaching out with your holy gospel.

Blessed be the narthex and entrance, that all who enter into this space might feel that this is a holy place, a loving and caring place.

Blessed be the space that is used for education, that it might resound with the Good News of the gospel of Jesus.

Blessed be the space for fellowship, that people might care and inquire about one another and that friendship in Christ might prosper.

Blessed be the space for offices, that those who work there might know the peace of the Lord and be effective in leadership and guidance.

Blessed be the increased sanctuary space, that we might continue and increase in spiritual hunger for Word and sacrament. Lord, in your mercy,

PEOPLE: Hear our prayer.

MINISTER: All your works praise you, O Lord.

PEOPLE: And your faithful servants bless you.

MINISTER: Blessed are you, O Lord our God, king of the universe. Your gifts are many and in wisdom you have made all things to give you glory. Be with us now and bless us as we dedicate this building to your praise and honor. Give us joy in all your works, and grant that this building may always be a place where your will is done and your name is glorified.

PEOPLE: Amen.

MINISTER: Now let this site and building be consecrated to the Lord, to his kingdom's use, and to his glory, in the name of the Father, and of the Son, and of the Holy Spirit.

PEOPLE: Amen.

MINISTER: Let us bless the Lord.

PEOPLE: Thanks be to God.

MINISTER: The blessings of almighty God, the Father, the Son, and the Holy Spirit be with you all.

PEOPLE: Amen.

MINISTER: The peace of the Lord be with you.

PEOPLE: And also with you.

Our Saviour's Lutheran Church
Naperville, Illinois
Gerald W. Nelson, pastor

Litany of Dedication of the Building Committee

LEADER: We come this morning to dedicate and set apart these persons serving on our building committee. We are thankful for their dedication and faithfulness.

PEOPLE: We are thankful for their willingness to serve. We pledge our support for this committee and promise to pray for them as they work for the church, for God, and for us.

COMMITTEE'S RESPONSE: We understand that the congregation has entrusted us with this position of responsibility. Through prayer and work we will seek to be faithful in fulfilling our duties.

LEADER: Know in this endeavor that "God [is] with us" (Matt. 1:23). As we work and plan for our new facility, we must be mindful of the Scripture:

Unless the LORD builds the house,
those who build it labor in vain (Ps. 127:1).

PEOPLE: We are thankful for the Spirit's presence in the life of our congregation. Our new sanctuary will be built with God's help and in God's name.

LEADER: We think of the song "The Church's One Foundation." May love always be the mortar with which we build the church and our lives.

ALL IN UNISON: As we dedicate and commit our building committee to its task, we also rededicate our lives to the work and ministry of Jesus Christ. We pray that we might be unyielding in love, tireless in service, and faithful in commitment.

Taylor Lake Christian Church
Seabrook, Texas
Dale Walling, pastor

Reading for the Dedication of a Chapel

TRUSTEES: We present this chapel to be dedicated to the glory of God and the service of all people.

MINISTER: By what name shall this chapel be known?

TRUSTEES: It shall be called the _____.

MINISTER: To the glory of God the Father who has called us by his grace; to the honor of his Son who loved us and gave himself for us; to the praise of the Holy Spirit who illumines and sanctifies us,

PEOPLE: We dedicate this chapel.

MINISTER: For the worship of God in prayer and praise, for the preaching of the everlasting gospel, for the celebration of the holy sacraments,

PEOPLE: We dedicate this chapel.

MINISTER: For the comfort of all who mourn, for hope and strength to those who are tempted, for light to those who seek the way,

PEOPLE: We dedicate this chapel.

MINISTER: For the hallowing of family life, for teaching and guiding the young, for the perfecting of the saints,

PEOPLE: We dedicate this chapel.

MINISTER: For the conversion of sinners, for the promotion of righteousness, for the extension of the kingdom of God,

PEOPLE: We dedicate this chapel.

MINISTER: In the unity of the faith, in the bond of Christian brotherhood, in charity and goodwill to all,

PEOPLE: We dedicate this chapel.

MINISTER: In gratitude for the labors of all who love and serve this church, in loving memory of the faithful members of this church who have been called to their reward but hoped and prayed for the completion of the church in their day,

PEOPLE: We dedicate this chapel.

ALL: We the people of this church and congregation, compassed about with a great cloud of witnesses, grateful for our heritage, aware of the sacrifice of our fathers in the faith, confessing that apart from us their work cannot be made perfect, do now dedicate ourselves anew to the worship and service of almighty God, through Jesus Christ our Lord. Amen.

MINISTER: Grant, O Lord, that all who here share in the sacraments, the ministry of the Word, and the fellowship of praise, may know that God is in this place, may hear your voice within their hearts, and may go forth to extend to the uttermost bounds of life the Lord Christ's kingdom. Amen.

Michigan Street United Methodist Church
Indianapolis, Indiana
R. M. Criswell, pastor

Litany for the Dedication of Chimes or Carillon (based on the Book of Psalms)

MINISTER: Inasmuch as we are bidden in sacred Scriptures to make a joyful noise unto the Lord and to serve the Lord with gladness and to come before his presence with singing, because the Lord is God, and he is the one who has made us and not we ourselves, we therefore acknowledge that we are indeed his people, the sheep of his pasture.

PEOPLE: Enter into his gates with thanksgiving and into his courts with praise; be thankful unto him and bless his name. For the Lord is good, his mercy is everlasting, and his truth endures to all generations. Therefore, to him we dedicate these chimes.

MINISTER: And because God's people in past generations have praised him, we in our day would also praise him. Praise the Lord, praise him in his sanctuary, praise him according to his excellent greatness. Yes, let everything that has breath praise the Lord.

PEOPLE: And to his praise and glory we dedicate these chimes.

MINISTER: And on the Lord's day, the day set aside and ordained for Christian worship, and so observed by the early disciples of our Lord, to remind the people of our city that this is the day of worship, and that it is well to enter God's house and there give praise and glory unto him who is the creator of life itself, and the giver of all good and perfect gifts,

PEOPLE: To his praise and to his glory we dedicate these church chimes.

MINISTER: And in the hour of sickness, trial, or temptation, it is our fond hope and earnest prayer that these church chimes, known for their sweet, tonal music, shall send forth their lovely musical strains, bringing fresh hope and renewed strength to those who for some reason may at that very moment be passing through the valley of the shadow of death,

PEOPLE: We dedicate these church chimes.

MINISTER: And inasmuch as music is the "universal language," the language of the soul, from day to day, week to week, month to month, and year to year, may these church chimes send forth their message. Set to music, they call, call all—the rich and the poor, the young and the old, the strong and the weak—to come to the house of the living God, where all may find grace and forgiveness through our blessed Lord and Savior, Jesus Christ, and strength to help and sustain them in the hour of need.

PEOPLE: To him be praise and glory forevermore. To his majesty who now sits on the throne of his glory in the eternal city whose builder and maker is God, we dedicate these church chimes.

First Christian Church
Grand Island, Nebraska
R.E. Yelderman, pastor

A Prayer of Dedication for New Choir Robes and Stoles

MINISTER: For the praise of almighty God with the voice of melody and jubilant anthem,

PEOPLE: We give you thanks, O God.

MINISTER: For the devotion of our choir, our director, and our organist,

PEOPLE: We give you thanks, O God.

MINISTER: For the commitment and generosity of choir members and others who love music,

PEOPLE: We give you thanks, O God.

MINISTER: For the beauty and harmony of sight with sound,

PEOPLE: We dedicate these new choir robes and colorful stoles to the glory of God.

MINISTER: For the symbol of your call to ministry represented by these stoles and for the life of _____ whom they memorialize,

PEOPLE: We give you thanks, O God.

MINISTER: May our ministry of music be enhanced, may our leadership in worship be increased, and may our music always give glory to God.

PEOPLE: O God of majesty and harmony, we dedicate to your praise and glory these new choir robes and stoles.

Arden Christian Church
Sacramento, California
C. Earl Gibbs, pastor

Litany for the Dedication of a Communion Cup

MINISTER: To Christ, who is our Savior and our Lord,

PEOPLE: We dedicate this cup, which is called a chalice, because it is directed to holy use.

MINISTER: This is the cup of remembrance. When it is used, we will remember the last meal our Lord had with his disciples, in which a cup was passed from one to the other as our Lord said, "Do this in remembrance of me" (*see* Luke 22:19).

PEOPLE: May this cup always help us remember that event, O Lord.

MINISTER: This is the cup of agony, and our use of it will cause us to recall our Lord's agony in Gethsemane, when he prayed, "My Father, if thou art willing, remove this cup from me" (Luke 22:42). And we will remember that sometimes God calls us to agony.

PEOPLE: May this thought ever be in our minds, O Lord.

MINISTER: This is the cup of dedication, and when we use it we will offer ourselves to drink from the cup of faith, allowing our Lord to lead us, and we will not hold back.

PEOPLE: Help us to make this a true promise, O Lord.

MINISTER: This is the cup of forgiveness. Each time that we see it, we ask to be moved to seek your forgiveness, O God.

PEOPLE: And we ask for the ability to forgive others.

MINISTER: This is the cup of fellowship, as people have been brought into loving togetherness when receiving its contents.

PEOPLE: And so, O Lord, may we be drawn closer together each time this cup is used.

MINISTER: To these purposes we consecrate this chalice, in memory of your devoted servant _____.

PEOPLE: Amen.

Salem United Church of Christ
Evansville, Indiana

Form for Use in the Laying of a Cornerstone

Call to Worship

Our help is in the name of the Lord, who made heaven and earth. Except the Lord build the house, they labor in vain that build it. Other foundations can no one lay than that is laid, which is Jesus Christ. Glory be to the Father, and to the Son, and to the Holy Spirit; as it was in the beginning, and ever shall be, world without end. Amen.

Prayer of Invocation

O Lord, exalted above the heavens, look down in the abundance of your goodness on us assembled in this place where we purpose to build a temple for the spiritual worship which becomes your holy name. Bless that which we did, that in all our works begun, continued, and ended in you, we may glorify your holy name, and finally by your mercy obtain everlasting life, through Jesus Christ our Lord. Amen.

Introductory Prayer for the Laying of the Cornerstone

O Lord Jesus Christ, Son of the living God, true cornerstone, immutable foundation, establish this stone which we plant in your holy name. You are the beginning and the ending, in whom all things were created. Bless our work, done for your service, that it may be carried on and perfected, to the praise and glory of your holy name, who, with the Father and the Holy Spirit, lives and reigns, one God, world without end. Amen.

Laying of the Cornerstone

In the name of the Father, and of the Son, and of the Holy Spirit, we lay this cornerstone to be erected under the name of (insert name of congregation) and devoted to the worship of almighty God. "Behold, I lay in Sion a chief corner stone" (1 Peter 2:6 KJV).

In this place may the faith flourish. Here may the voice of prayer continually be heard, the voice of rejoicing and salvation, the voice of praise and invocation of God's most glorious and honorable names, the name of the Father, and of the Son, and of the Holy Spirit, henceforth and forever. Amen.

Prayer of Dedication

Almighty and everlasting God, who has built the living temple of your church upon the foundation of the apostles and prophets, Jesus Christ himself being the chief cornerstone, we beseech you to prosper this work of our hands, which we have undertaken for the upbuilding of your kingdom and the glory of your church. To this end establish this stone which we now place in your name.

Blessed be you, O Lord God, who have put it into the hearts of your servants to build a house in which you may be worshiped, your gospel preached, and your holy sacraments administered for the comfort and salvation of all people.

O God, be pleased to accept the humble offering of your servants and fulfill the desires of their hearts. Shield and defend those who labor with their hands on this building, that there be continuing nurture of love. Grant to them, and to all here present, that all our service may be sacrificed and we may become in soul and body living temples of the Holy Spirit. All this we ask through the abundant merits of our Lord and Savior, who lives and reigns with you and the Holy Spirit, and who taught us to pray, saying (pray the Lord's Prayer).

Knox Presbyterian Church
Godorich, Ontario, Canada

Litany and Readings for a Cross-lifting Ceremony

READER: Matthew 5:14–16, John 3:14–17, Philippians 2:8–11

MINISTER: In a world where there is so much evil and in the hearts of people so much sin, the cross of Christ stands as an everlasting sign of God's suffering love and plan of redemption. No other symbol of the Christian religion has the significance and meaning to Christians, and none other is so precious as the cross.

We meet here to lift this cross to the crowning position on this church building, to place it at the top of the majestic spire.

In order that this house may be distinguished and marked as a house of Christian worship,

PEOPLE: We lift up this cross.

MINISTER: May this cross stand as a sentinel to remind people that "God so loved the world, that he gave his only begotten Son, that whosoever believeth in him should not perish, but have everlasting life" (John 3:16 KJV).

PEOPLE: We lift up this cross.

MINISTER: That Christ may be lifted up, his way exalted among people, and his message made known to everyone,

PEOPLE: We lift up this cross.

MINISTER: That all who see this house may be conscious of the cross as a symbol of our Christian faith, and that it may turn people's minds toward God and open their hearts to Christ,

PEOPLE: We lift up this cross.

MINISTER: That it may be a constant and continuing invitation to all people to come to the house of the Lord to worship,

PEOPLE: We lift up this cross.

MINISTER: That this cross on the top of the house of the Lord may be a reminder that it is the changeless symbol of our salvation, that people beholding the light of this cross may be turned from the way of darkness into the way of light,

PEOPLE: We lift up this cross.

MINISTER: That its shining radiance and reflective power may be a constant invitation to all people to come to the light and life which we may have through him who died on the cross,

PEOPLE: We lift up this cross.

MINISTER: That the light of our lives may not be kept under a bushel, but that our light may shine

before all people, that they may see our good works
and give glory to our Father who is in heaven,

PEOPLE: We lift up this cross.

MINISTER: That all people may know him whom to
know is life eternal,

PEOPLE: We dedicate this cross.

Congregational Christian Church
Lanett, Alabama
Joe A. French, pastor

A Litany for the Dedication of New Church Doors

MINISTER: That these portals may remind us of him who said, "I am the door: by me if any [person] enter in, [that person] shall be saved" (John 10:9 KJV),

PEOPLE: We pray to you, our Father.

MINISTER: That we may remember the words of Jesus who said, "Behold, I stand at the door, and knock; if any[one] hear my voice, and open the door, I will come in to [that person], and will [eat] with him, and he with me" (Rev. 3:20 KJV).

PEOPLE: We pray to you, dear God.

MINISTER: For the skill and craftsmanship of design of the doors which offer entrance to this house of worship,

PEOPLE: We thank you, Lord.

MINISTER: That these doors may always open to denote unhindered access to our worship of you, God, the Father, Son, and Holy Spirit,

PEOPLE: We pray to you, Lord.

MINISTER: That all who enter these doors may find solace for grief, stimulation for intellect, joy for mourning, tranquility for turmoil; for all who seek you, the faithful and the doubting,

PEOPLE: We pray to you, good Lord.

MINISTER: That the memory of those who have gone before us and those present who have made possible these graceful and enduring portals for your house and the glory of your holy name may be remembered among us,

PEOPLE: We pray to you, Lord.

MINISTER: That these doors may never be closed to needs of any kind, but swing out to declare your love and our willingness to serve,

PEOPLE: We pray to you, dear Lord.

MINISTER: To the honor and glory of the Father, Son, and Holy Spirit,

PEOPLE: We dedicate these doors, O Lord. Amen.

Stanley Anderson
St. Louis, Missouri

Dedication of Financial Pledges

MINISTER: During the past few days messengers from your church have called at your homes, presenting the program of the church for the next year. They have given each of you an opportunity to express your intentions of sharing in that program. We have now come to the time when those who have pledged should be publicly dedicated, together with their commitments to this program.

PEOPLE: We give you but your own, whatever the gift may be; all that we have is yours alone, a trust, O Lord, from you.

MINISTER: As you have chosen us, O God, and enriched our lives,

PEOPLE: We offer ourselves, our talents, and our substance to you.

MINISTER: To the ministry of the gospel, the inspiration of sacred music, the singing of the hymns of the ages,

PEOPLE: We offer ourselves, our talents, and our substance to you.

MINISTER: To the Christian education of children, to the guidance of youth, and to the spiritual security and renewal of those of mature years,

PEOPLE: We offer ourselves, our talents, and our substance to you.

MINISTER: To the Christian character of our city, the spirit of tolerance and goodwill,

PEOPLE: We offer ourselves, our talents, and our substance to you.

MINISTER: For the Christianization of the world, the economic and spiritual elevation of untold millions,

PEOPLE: We offer ourselves, our talents, and our substance to you.

MINISTER: Looking for that day when the spirit of Christ shall clothe itself in the hearts of our age, and swords shall be beaten into plowshares, and peace shall cover the world,

PEOPLE: We offer ourselves, our talents, and our substance to you.

MINISTER: Let us pray. Almighty and everlasting God, you have given us life, Christian homes, indeed, all that we have. Accept the gifts which symbolize the giving of our lives. Transform the gold from our purses into programs which enlarge our vision and strengthen our church. Seeking the happiness of children, the stimulus of youthful ideas, and the assurance of the rewards of righteousness, we pray in Jesus' name. Amen.

First Congregational Church
Warrenton, Iowa
Charles F. Jacobs, pastor

Recognition
of Former
Pastors

MINISTER: For those who are charged with the conduct of worship, the guidance of souls, and their religious experiences and needs,

PEOPLE: We give you thanks, O God.

MINISTER: For all such trusted interpreters of your message to human life, and particularly for the first pastors of this congregation for giving the continuing consciousness of your sustaining and enlightening presence,

PEOPLE: We give you thanks, O God.

MINISTER: Continue to bless them with health, activity, and the joy of doing your holy task,

PEOPLE: O Lord, we beseech you.

MINISTER: For these pastors who confirmed our faith, rebuked our sins, testified to the simplicity of the life that is in Christ, and pointed to that high way,

PEOPLE: O Lord, we give you thanks.

MINISTER: For their careful administration of the means of grace, their good and faithful interpretation of the Word, their ardent teaching of your truth, their faithful visitation of the people, and their careful counseling of those in trouble and in sorrow,

PEOPLE: O Lord, we give you thanks.

MINISTER: O holy Father, give them the joy which is reserved for those who are dedicated to your service, the knowledge that they made plain to others the way which has been hard to find,

PEOPLE: O Lord, we beseech you.

MINISTER: For those who came not to be ministered unto, but to minister, and gave their lives in service for many,

PEOPLE: O Lord, we give you thanks.

Lakewood Presbyterian Church
Cleveland, Ohio
L. Wilson Kilgore, pastor

Litany for the Dedication of a Funeral Pall

MINISTER: Let us pray. God of life and Lord of death, we come now to dedicate this funeral pall to your glory and in memory of _____. For the gift of your Son Jesus Christ who revealed you to us as a loving, heavenly Father,

PEOPLE: We give you praise, O God.

MINISTER: For the words of eternal life and his teaching that he came that we might have life and have it abundantly,

PEOPLE: We give you praise, O God.

MINISTER: For the promise of Jesus: "I am the resurrection and the life; he who believes in me, though he die, yet shall he live, and whoever lives and believes in me shall never die" (John 11:25–26),

PEOPLE: We lift up our hearts in thanksgiving.

MINISTER: For the assurance that your people never perish, and no one shall snatch them out of the Father's hand,

PEOPLE: We lift up our hearts in thanksgiving.

MINISTER: For the gift of your Spirit who gives life and guides us in all truth,

PEOPLE: We lift up our hearts in thanksgiving.

MINISTER: As we dedicate this pall, we praise you and thank you for the good news of forgiveness from you, acceptance by you, and fellowship with you now and forever. O God, our Lord and Savior, we dedicate ourselves anew in gratitude to you and to those who have gone before us—who loved you and served you and followed you. By your Spirit renew our spirits, and give us a deeper dedication to do your will. Help us to glorify you that we may enjoy you in this life and in the life everlasting; in the name of the Father, and the Son, and the Holy Spirit. Amen.

Caldwell Memorial Presbyterian Church
Charlotte, North Carolina
Charles I. Kirby, pastor

Reading for a Ground-breaking Ceremony

MINISTER: For the people who organized this congregation in the pioneer days of this community and who guided its destinies through those early and difficult years,

PEOPLE: We express our heartfelt thanks, O God.

MINISTER: For all those in the past who were responsible for planning and providing our first house of worship on another location, and then our present church building here,

PEOPLE: We express our heartfelt thanks, O God.

MINISTER: For all those present here, and all other members of our church family who are away or have been taken by death, who have thought and planned and given of themselves for this worthy project,

PEOPLE: We express our heartfelt thanks, O God.

MINISTER: For many who have labored in raising funds and for all who have given with generosity and cheerfulness,

PEOPLE: We express our heartfelt thanks, O God.

MINISTER: For those who have designed this structure, and for all by whose hands and skill and toil this building will be completed,

PEOPLE: We express our heartfelt thanks, O God.

MINISTER: So that the building to be erected here will provide a place of beauty for our children to learn more about Jesus and his life,

PEOPLE: We ask your blessing on it, dear Lord.

MINISTER: So that it may give teachers of the children a more adequate place to work,

PEOPLE: We ask your blessing on it, dear Lord.

MINISTER: So that it may be used for strengthening and building your kingdom here on earth in every way,

PEOPLE: We ask your blessing on it, dear Lord.

MINISTER: And from these moments of gratitude and blessing we are led into moments of renewed dedication. To its use for the sacred purpose for which it is now set aside,

PEOPLE: We dedicate this ground, our heavenly Father.

MINISTER: All the labor that will be put into this building,

PEOPLE: We dedicate as a service to you, our heavenly Father.

MINISTER: And finally, our highest hopes and fondest dreams for the future of our church and our very lives,

PEOPLE: We dedicate to you, our heavenly Father. Amen.

MINISTER: Heavenly Father, we invoke your blessing as we meet for this service of dedication. May your Spirit guide us and your presence be evident to us as we seek to prepare ourselves for our spiritual ministry. Grant our prayer in Jesus' name. Amen.

First Congregational Church
Grand Blanc, Michigan
Donald A. Wenstrom, pastor

Senior Home Ground-breaking Ceremony

MINISTER: Your hands have made and fashioned me. Give me understanding that I may learn your commandments. They that fear you will be glad when they see me, because I have hoped in your Word.

PEOPLE: Let, I pray you, God, your merciful kindness be my comfort, according to your Word to your servant. Let your tender mercies come to me, that I may live; for your law is my delight.

MINISTER: "Except the LORD build the house, they labour in vain that build it: except the LORD keep the city, the watchman waketh but in vain" (Ps. 127:1 KJV).

PEOPLE: Jesus said: "Then the King will say to those at his right hand, Come, O blessed of my Father, inherit the kingdom prepared for you from the foundation of the world; for I was hungry and you gave me food, I was thirsty and you gave me drink, I was a stranger and you welcomed me" (Matt. 25:34–35).

MINISTER: And Jacob took the stone which he had under his head and poured oil upon it and called it Bethel, which means, "the house of God" (see Gen. 28:18–19).

PEOPLE: And he said, "This stone, which I have set up for a pillar, shall be God's house" (v. 22).

MINISTER: In the name of God the Father, God the Son, and God the Holy Spirit,

PEOPLE: We dedicate this ground.

MINISTER: So that a new building may be erected on it which will provide for the elderly a home of comfort and peace,

PEOPLE: We dedicate this ground.

MINISTER: So that those who serve through this place might be inspired by your love and encouraged by your wisdom in providing Christian care and that those residing here may be enriched by the evidence of your concern,

PEOPLE: We dedicate this ground and give praise to God.

MINISTER: That there might be found among those members of our community who enter into this fellowship a haven of love which shall shine forth as a beacon showing God's concern for all,

PEOPLE: We dedicate this ground and glorify God.

First Presbyterian Church
Cambridge, New York
William G. Doxsey, pastor

Litany and Prayers for the Dedication of a Hospital

MINISTER: In the name of the Father, and of the Son, and of the Holy Spirit.

PEOPLE: Amen.

MINISTER: Our help is in the name of the Lord,

PEOPLE: Who made heaven and earth.

MINISTER: Our Lord Jesus said, "Come unto me, all ye that labour and are heavy laden, and I will give you rest" (Matt. 11:28 KJV).

PEOPLE: "Take my yoke upon you, and learn of me; for I am meek and lowly in heart: and ye shall find rest unto your souls" (v. 29).

MINISTER: When it was evening, they brought to him many people that were possessed, and he cast out the spirits with his word and healed all that were sick,

PEOPLE: That it might be fulfilled which was spoken by Isaiah the prophet, saying, He took upon himself our infirmities and bare our sicknesses (see Matt. 8:16–17).

MINISTER: The Lord is close to all who call upon him, to all that call upon him in truth. He will fulfill the desire of them that fear him, he also will hear their cry, and will save them. The Lord be with you.

PEOPLE: And with your spirit.

MINISTER: Blest and dedicated be this building to the glory of God and the ministry of love and healing care, in the name of the Father, and of the Son, and of the Holy Spirit. Amen.

Inasmuch as you have done it unto one of the least of these my brethren, you have done it unto me (see Matt. 25:40).

Hallowed also be this building (and the gifts thereto) to the honor and memory of those beloved of the donors.

Bear one another's burdens and so fulfill the law of Christ. The memory of the just is blessed.

Let us pray.

O Lord God, our compassionate and merciful heavenly Father, who heals all our diseases and comforts us in all our distresses, and who does commit your suffering children to our loving care and ministry, be pleased to accept at our hands this building, reared in your name to your glory, to be a harbor and resting place for those troubled with sickness. Of your mercy, we ask you, put upon it and all that is done here to relieve and cure the distresses of body and mind, your healing benediction, so that thanksgiving may rise to glorify you who is our health and our song, through Jesus Christ, our Savior. Amen.

Let us pray for all who may be brought to this house of mercy.

O God, our Father, whose compassion never fails,

whose love always guards us, whose presence always aids us, hear us, we humbly ask, when we pray for all who may ever come here seeking health, and grant that they may find both health of body and the healing medicine of your saving grace, through Jesus Christ, our Lord. Amen.

Let us pray for all who minister here.

Most merciful Father, who commits to our love and care our fellow human beings in their necessities, graciously be with and prosper all those who are seeking and ministering to the sick and needy, especially those who are serving in this place. Let their ministry be abundantly blessed in bringing ease to the suffering, comfort to the sorrowing, and peace to the dying, and let their lives be inspired with the consecration of selfless service, knowing that inasmuch as they do it even to the least of the master's children, they do it to him who came to minister your love to people, even your Son, Jesus Christ, our Lord. Amen.

Let us pray for all who in this place will cry to our Father.

Almighty and everlasting God, the comfort of the sad, the strength of sufferers, let the prayers of those who cry out of any tribulation come to you, that they may rejoice to find your mercy is present with them in their affliction, through Jesus Christ our Lord. Amen.

Let us pray as our Lord has taught us to pray, for each other and for ourselves. (In unison, pray the Lord's Prayer.)

Carlsbad Union Church
Carlsbad, California
Roy D. Brokenshire, pastor

Reading for Dedication of Hymnals

MINISTER: "O sing unto the LORD a new song: sing unto the LORD, all the earth."

PEOPLE: "Sing unto the LORD, bless his name, shew forth his salvation from day to day."

MINISTER: "Declare his glory among the heathen, his wonders among all people."

PEOPLE: "For the LORD is great, and greatly to be praised: he is to be feared above all gods" (Ps. 96:1–4 KJV).

MINISTER: To the glory of God, the author of praise,

PEOPLE: We dedicate these hymnals.

MINISTER: To the memory of loved ones and with gratitude for each donor,

PEOPLE: We dedicate these hymnals.

MINISTER: We also dedicate these hymnals as a means of expressing our faith.

PEOPLE: [Communicate with one another] "in psalms and hymns and spiritual songs, singing and making melody in your heart to the Lord" (Eph. 5:19 KJV).

MINISTER: We also dedicate these hymnals as a means to Christian growth.

PEOPLE: "Teaching and admonishing one another in psalms and hymns and spiritual songs, singing with grace in your hearts to the Lord" (Col. 3:16 KJV).

ALL: We dedicate these hymnals and promise to sing songs of praise to the Lord until all the ends of the earth shall see and hear the salvation of our God.

Chinese Department
Flagler Street Baptist Church
Miami, Florida

Litany for Dedication of a Kneeling Bench and Candelabra

MINISTER: God of Abraham, Isaac, and Jacob, God of our fathers and our God,

PEOPLE: We dedicate these articles to be used in worship to the glory of God.

MINISTER: Jesus said, "I am the light of the world."

PEOPLE: "He who follows me will not walk in darkness, but will have the light of life" (John 8:12).

MINISTER: God is light and in him is no darkness at all. If we walk in the light, as he is the light,

PEOPLE: We have fellowship with one another, and the blood of Jesus his Son cleanses us from all sin.

MINISTER: Jesus said, "You are the light of the world."

PEOPLE: "Let your light so shine before [others] that they may see your good works and give glory to your Father who is in heaven" (Matt. 5:16).

ALL: Glory be to the Father, and to the Son, and to the Holy Spirit. Amen.

Prayer of Dedication

MINISTER: O Holy Savior, you are the light of the world, you are a light for our path and a lamp for our feet. We come before you to dedicate these candelabra and this kneeling bench. We bow before you, O Lord, of whom it has been declared "that at the name of Jesus every knee should bow . . . and every tongue confess that Jesus Christ is Lord, to the glory of God the Father" (Phil. 2:10–11). We hold these vessels before you that they may be set apart as instruments of your light, your peace, and your love. You have created all things for your glory and you have commanded us to have no other gods before you. We bow before you on bended knee to pledge these pieces to the use of this congregation, and the people of God who follow them, to celebrate the gifts of light, wisdom, prayer, love, joy, and peace. We ask your blessing on those who use them, that their lives may be joined together in love for you and for one another; may your presence go with them to light their way not only in their worship, but also in all that they do for your glory. In the name of the Father, and the Son, and the Holy Spirit. Amen.

Caldwell Memorial Presbyterian Church
Charlotte, North Carolina
Charles L. Kirby, pastor

Litany for Dedication of Amplified Lectern

MINISTER: To the glory of God, author of all goodness and beauty, who blesses us with endless blessings,

PEOPLE: We dedicate this lectern.

MINISTER: Remembering that Jesus often admonished those to whom he ministered, "He who has ears to hear, let him hear" (Matt. 11:15),

PEOPLE: We dedicate this lectern that all may hear more easily.

MINISTER: Recognizing that in this world so much misunderstanding between people is the result of not having heard aright or communicated adequately,

PEOPLE: We dedicate this lectern to the end that our words may be clear and easily discerned.

MINISTER: In gratitude to God who in his infinite love sent his only Son into the world as the living Word to speak to all people his words of life,

PEOPLE: We dedicate this lectern.

MINISTER: That we may more easily communicate the gospel and hear it more distinctly,

PEOPLE: We dedicate this lectern.

MINISTER: That we may hear the cries for help more easily as programs are presented concerning the hurts and needs of God's children everywhere,

PEOPLE: We dedicate this lectern.

MINISTER: In loving memory of _____ who loved and served God in many ways and witnessed well to (his/her) faith, and who loved Christ's church,

PEOPLE: We dedicate this lectern.

MINISTER: Let us pray together:

ALL: Almighty God, who from ancient times has put it into the hearts of your people to make offerings for your service and for the use of your church, and who has been pleased at all times to accept the gifts of their hands, we ask you to accept this memorial, which we have now set apart in your name and to your glory. May your blessings rest on those who have made this gift and on all those who shall benefit from its use. We give you thanks for your servants in whose memory these gifts have been given, and we praise you for their witness of faith and their faithfulness in service. We ask this all in the name of Jesus Christ our Lord, who lives and reigns with you and the Holy Spirit, world without end. Amen.

First Presbyterian Church
Fort Scott, Kansas
Gordon I. Zimmerman, pastor

Reading for the Merging of Congregations

READER: Psalm 133

MINISTER: (Ministers of each congregation may alternate in reading the Litany.) Many times in Scripture our Lord Jesus Christ urged the coming together of brothers and sisters united in him. Today we accomplish the merger of (insert name of congregation) and (insert name of congregation). Let us consecrate ourselves to the fulfillment of his purposes. To all who have had a part in bringing this happy occasion to come about, we express our thanks. Let us now consecrate ourselves as a new community of Christians.

MINISTER: To the glory of God, our Father and Creator,

PEOPLE: We dedicate ourselves.

MINISTER: For the guidance of our children and youth in the Christian way of life and instruction in righteousness,

PEOPLE: We dedicate ourselves.

MINISTER: To comfort those who mourn, to strengthen those who are tempted, to help those who persevere,

PEOPLE: We dedicate ourselves.

MINISTER: In grateful remembrance of those who went before us, in gratitude for labors and sacrifices, to the forwarding of their principles of freedom under God,

PEOPLE: We dedicate ourselves.

MINISTER: To the well-being of the living, to the renunciation of evil, to the aid of the weak and of the strong, of the rich, and of the poor,

PEOPLE: We dedicate ourselves.

MINISTER: To the publicizing of the truth, to the liberty of the children of God, to respect for the worthy past, to acceptance of the future good,

PEOPLE: We dedicate ourselves.

MINISTER: To the integrity of the family, the guidance of childhood, the fellowship of friends,

PEOPLE: We dedicate ourselves.

MINISTER: To noble toil for this community, to promotion of civic righteousness, to the consecration of all earthly powers to God's glory,

PEOPLE: We dedicate ourselves.

ALL: Seeing we are encompassed about with so great a cloud of witnesses, we declare and consecrate ourselves as the (insert name of new congregation) to serve our God and his Son, even Jesus Christ, in this place and indeed throughout the world.

MINISTER: Hear Christ's prayer for us: John 17:11–26.

Norman L. Hersey
Publisher, Church Management

Prayer for the Retirement of a Mortgage Debt

MINISTER: We are here, O God, to establish our place in history, to rejoice in reaching a milestone in the satisfaction of the indebtedness on this building, and to set our minds on new dreams in a continuing journey.

PEOPLE: Accept our joy and give us new vision.

MINISTER: We do not come alone. We come here with the cloud of saints and witnesses who have gone before us, who have led us in ministry by faithful example in the stewardship of their whole lives.

PEOPLE: They are the historic saints of centuries of the kingdom of God; they are our friends, our family, our mothers and fathers; they are the ones who have established the church that meets in this building.

MINISTER: All of our days have not been easy. Within the life of the congregation, we have been called to be strong, to sacrifice, to realign priorities, and to remain faithful when faith is weak.

PEOPLE: We confess that the life of service is difficult, that the road to life is not easy, that true service and maturity require that we die to gain life.

MINISTER: As we have sacrificed to make this moment possible, we have also been given life as we have labored in dedicated service.

PEOPLE: We continue to commit ourselves to the service of the church and to reach around the world in ministry.

MINISTER: "For God so loved the world that he gave his only Son, that whoever believes in him should not perish but have eternal life" (John 3:16).

PEOPLE: "Go therefore and make disciples of all nations, baptizing them in the name of the Father and of the Son and of the Holy Spirit" (Matt. 28:19).

MINISTER: Accept now our joy in this milestone of accomplishment in the fulfillment of our obligation on the mortgage-note indebtedness on this building.

PEOPLE: And accept also our rededicated lives to this sharing of the gospel with the world.

Central Christian Church
Granite City, Illinois
V. Dennis Rutledge, pastor

Dedication of Office Equipment (Computer, Copier)

MINISTER: It is indeed fitting and proper that we dedicate this office equipment. The work of the church is becoming increasingly complex and it is incumbent on us to "redeem the time"—to make the most of our time that we may be witnesses to the gospel of Jesus Christ.

MINISTER: To the glory of God,

PEOPLE: We dedicate this office equipment.

MINISTER: To the memory of _____,

PEOPLE: We dedicate this office equipment.

MINISTER: That the work of Jesus Christ in the church may be performed more efficiently and effectively,

PEOPLE: We dedicate this office equipment to your honor and glory. Amen.

MINISTER: We thank you, our Father and our God, that you have provided machines that would make our work lighter. We thank you for the one we memorialize through this piece of office equipment today. We pray that your work may be accomplished more efficiently and effectively as we use every opportunity to be of service to your holy name. Amen.

First Presbyterian Church
Lakewood, New Jersey
Gordon Shelley, pastor

Dedication of Organ and Chimes

The Prelude

The Hymn: "Praise to the Lord, the Almighty"

The Prayer

A Litany of Praise

MINISTER: Sing to the Lord a new song, he has done wonderful things!

PEOPLE: Sing for joy to the Lord, all the earth!

MINISTER: Praise him with songs and shouts of joy!

PEOPLE: Sing praises to the Lord! Play music on the organ!

MINISTER: Blow trumpets and horns,

PEOPLE: And shout for joy to the Lord!

A Prayer of Thanksgiving

ALL: Our Lord and God, we thank you for this day you have made. We thank you for all the people whom you have loved and given us to love. We thank you for the gifts of song and organ and chimes with which we may voice our praise. Bless us, O God, and help us to learn to be grateful, responsible, and loving.

May we become more fully aware of and responsive to your greatest gift of all: your love made visible to us through Jesus Christ. Amen.

Presentation of the Organ and Chimes

MINISTER: We present this organ and chimes to be dedicated to the glory of God, to the upbuilding of human life, and to the service of the church.

Responsive Act of Dedication

MINISTER: To the glory of God who calls us by his grace, to the honor of his Son, who loves us and gave himself for us, to the praise of the Holy Spirit who lives in us and recreates us, we dedicate this organ and chimes.

PEOPLE: Praise God in his sanctuary. Praise him in the firmament of his power. Praise him with the sound of trumpet; praise him with lute and harp.

MINISTER: We dedicate this organ and chimes to God for the proclamation of the gospel, the Good News; for the worship of God through music; for the nurture and instruction of children, youth, and adults in God's way of truth and love; for the expressing of the beauty of holiness; for the celebration of God's presence in the sanctuary and in all of life.

PEOPLE: Praise him with stringed instruments and organ! Let everything that has breath praise the Lord!

MINISTER: We dedicate this organ and chimes to the healing of life's discords and the revelation of the hidden soul of harmony; to the lifting up of the depressed and the comforting of the sorrowing; to the humbling of the heart before eternal mysteries and the lifting of the soul to abiding beauty and joy by the gospel of infinite love and goodwill.

PEOPLE: That at the name of Jesus every knee should bow, in heaven and on earth, and every tongue confess that Jesus Christ is Lord, to the glory of God the Father.

MINISTER: In thankfulness for the love so graciously expressed in sacrificial giving, in loving remembrance of those who have been memorialized; in gratitude for the labors of all who love and serve Christ through his church here and everywhere, we dedicate this organ and chimes.

PEOPLE: We, the people of this congregation, surrounded by a great cloud of witnesses, thankful for our heritage and sensitive to the sacrifices of those who have gone this way before us, dedicate ourselves anew to the worship and service of God through Jesus Christ our Lord. Amen.

Sounds of the Organ and Chimes

Benediction

Closing Hymn: "Now Thank We All Our God"

The Postlude

Prairie Avenue Christian Church
Decatur, Illinois
John L. Bray, pastor

Dedication
of a
Parking Lot

(The congregation will follow the minister out of the church building and onto the parking lot after the closing hymn.)

MINISTER: We stand on our new parking lot. It shall become for us a reminder of the dedication of our now-deceased members whose memorial it will remain.

PEOPLE: In gratitude for the financial gifts which have made this facility possible, we dedicate this lot.

MINISTER: We stand where in generations past our forebears tilled the soil and harvested food for their tables.

PEOPLE: We recognize the dedication of our forebears and our obligation to provide for others who will look upon us as their forebears, and to this purpose we dedicate this lot.

MINISTER: Often we choose to make decisions which affect the lives of others with little concern for the ultimate things of life.

PEOPLE: We dedicate this lot as part of our facilities, all of which will serve to enrich us when we worship and receive instruction.

MINISTER: We profess that our ultimate ministry is for our Lord Jesus Christ, and we confess that we have failed in so many ways to exercise that ministry faithfully.

PEOPLE: Help us, O Lord, to dedicate ourselves anew, along with this parking lot, in service to your holy name. Amen.

Prayer of Dedication

MINISTER: Indeed, O Lord, we are mindful of all the opportunities you place before us for ministry. Help us not to miss them. Help us to make accommodation in our facilities and our plant management which would allow for as many of your children as possible to be full participants in our life together at (insert name of congregation).

Again, for the lives of those who provided the financial support to construct this parking lot as well as for the dedication of those who worked so hard on its planning and its construction, for the labor of those who did the actual work of stoning, topping, sealing, and striping—for all these we give thanks to you for their hard work.

Bless, O Lord, our continued attempts at being faithful to your calling as the children of light. May our hearts and minds be open to the varieties of potential ministries which this lot may now represent.

We proceed to dedicate this lot in the name of the Father, the Son, and the Holy Spirit, as a reasonable gift in your service. Amen.

Depart in peace.

St. Peter's United Church of Christ
Amherst, Ohio
Joseph R. Foster, pastor

Dedication for Public School Educators

MINISTER: O God, you call us into your church to share the cost and joy of discipleship, but you also call us into the world.

ALL: When we consider the talents with which we have been blessed, we ask you to show us your calling for our lives.

MINISTER: Grant to your followers confidence and joy as they undertake a new school year.

EDUCATORS: Inspire in us patience, O Lord.

MINISTER: Whether they be behind the desk or in front of the chalkboard, grant them wisdom, humor, and comfort with their responsibilities.

EDUCATORS: Guide us to recognize the individual needs of those who have been entrusted to our care, O Lord.

MINISTER: You are from everlasting to everlasting, Lord, but when you came to earth you taught, and you supported your followers as you called them to teach.

ALL: Strengthen our faith. Teach us love. Show us your way. In Jesus' name we pray. Amen.

MINISTER: May you find renewal of faith through the work you do. God bless you.

Frieden's United Church of Christ
Sunneytown, Pennsylvania
Homer E. Royer, pastor

Reading for the Dedication of a Church Sign

MINISTER: We have gathered on this happy occasion to dedicate our new church sign.

PEOPLE: We know where this sign came from, but where did the word *sign* come from?

MINISTER: We remember the word *sign* from the Bible.

PEOPLE: How did people then react to signs?

MINISTER: In the New Testament the word *wonders* is, with one exception, always connected with the word *signs*.

PEOPLE: What kind of signs and wonders can we expect?

MINISTER: Actually, Jesus became a sign. We should think of him as God's significant revelation. In the Bible, a *sign* is said to confirm the word of God, it appeals to the sense of sight, and it serves as a visible indicator, which points to the invisible power and activity of God in the world.

PEOPLE: Then let this sign remind all who pass by of God's activity in this church and the world.

MINISTER: And more, it will serve as a beacon to let people know who we are and how important we think study and worship are. Will you be ready to accept those who see our sign and come?

PEOPLE: We are thankful that Christ has befriended us. We can do no less. We dedicate ourselves to Christ's mission.

ALL: With thankfulness for our tradition and with hope for the future, we dedicate this sign.

First United Methodist Church
Dexter, Missouri
David W. Richardson, pastor

Dedication of Stained-Glass Windows

Act of Acceptance

MINISTER: Acting on behalf of the congregation, I accept the gift of these beautiful memorial windows with appreciation to all who contributed toward their purchase.

Act of Dedication

MINISTER: With gratitude to those who have contributed these windows and in appreciation for the lives which are memorialized each time we see them,

PEOPLE: We accept these windows.

MINISTER: To the glory of God who inspired his children to bring the beauty of the rainbow into materials where it can be more frequently appreciated,

PEOPLE: We dedicate these gifts.

MINISTER: With devotion to our Lord Jesus Christ who has led us to know God and brought us the knowledge that in unity and in the light we may perform a higher service and more perfectly fulfill the will of God,

PEOPLE: We dedicate these windows.

MINISTER: For the artists and craftsmen whose hands fashioned and placed these windows, and whose skills and insights will eternally inspire those who worship here,

PEOPLE: We give you thanks, O God.

MINISTER: For those who, through the centuries, carried the message of the gospel through the world, in obedience to Christ's command,

PEOPLE: We praise your name, O God.

MINISTER: For the privilege which is ours, of being stewards of the gospel, workers who have no need to be ashamed, handling aright the Word of truth and passing it on to generations yet unborn,

PEOPLE: We praise your name, O God.

MINISTER: Almighty God, who has given, and who restores to us, those we delight to hold in memory, we recognize that you are the Creator of all things and in need of nothing, yet we desire to worship you in the sanctuary. Accept, we pray, the offering of these memorial windows and the lives which have been given to you in them; consecrate them by your power and blessing to holy use. May all who worship here now and in the years to come find inspiration in and through them and be lifted up toward you, the source of all being and beauty. This prayer we offer in the name of Jesus Christ our Lord. Amen.

Prairie Avenue Christian Church
Decatur, Illinois
John L. Bray, pastor

Service for the Dedication of a Steeple and Bell

Prelude

Processional Hymn: "Open Now Thy Gates of Beauty"

MINISTER: In the name of the Father, and of the Son, and of the Holy Spirit.

PEOPLE: Amen.

Responsive Reading

MINISTER: "I will lift up mine eyes unto the hills, from whence cometh my help."

PEOPLE: "My help cometh from the LORD which made heaven and earth."

MINISTER: "He will not suffer thy foot to be moved: he that keepeth thee will not slumber."

PEOPLE: "Behold, he that keepeth Israel will neither slumber nor sleep."

MINISTER: "The LORD is thy keeper, the LORD is thy shade upon thy right hand."

PEOPLE: "The sun shall not smite thee by day, nor the moon by night."

MINISTER: "The LORD shall preserve thee from all evil: he shall preserve thy soul."

ALL: The LORD shall preserve thy going out and thy coming in from this time forth, and even for evermore. Amen.

Anthem

Service of Dedication

MINISTER: Through the grace of God, we have come to this joyous occasion when the steeple and bell, which we have long desired, have become a reality. Now let us join in prayer, thanking God for his mercy, seeking his blessing and dedicating the steeple, the bell, and our lives to his holy purpose.

PEOPLE: "Our Father, who art in heaven, hallowed be thy name."

MINISTER: Accept the work of our hands expressed in this steeple and bell as we set them apart to do your work, and to honor and glorify your name.

PEOPLE: "Thy kingdom come. Thy will be done, on earth as it is in heaven."

MINISTER: May the ringing of this bell pierce into the wilderness of your lives, may it call you to worship, and may it provide refreshment for your souls.

PEOPLE: "Give us this day our daily bread. And forgive us our debts as we forgive our debtors."

MINISTER: May the steeple be your constant reminder to lift your eyes unto the hills. May it be your source of inspiration when trouble overwhelms you. And may its heavenward thrust make you continually aware of your need for prayer.

PEOPLE: "And lead us not into temptation, but deliver us from evil."

MINISTER: And as the construction of this steeple and bell is futile without the devotion of the people,

PEOPLE: We recommit our lives to you.

MINISTER: In grateful appreciation to our heavenly Father, through whose kindness, inspiration, and guidance we have come to the (insert year) anniversary of the ground-breaking of our church,

PEOPLE: We rededicate this house of prayer.

MINISTER: In gratitude for the honesty, industry, and integrity of those who have gone before us, and for the bountiful spirit of friendship and fellowship throughout this congregation,

PEOPLE: We rededicate our church today, with its steeple and bell, and we recommit our lives to the faithful service of Jesus Christ.

ALL: "For thine is the kingdom, and the power, and the glory, for ever. Amen."

MINISTER: Almighty and everlasting God, accept the offering of this our steeple and bell which we have erected to the glory of your holy name. Send down your Holy Spirit, we beseech you, and let this steeple and every part thereof be sanctified and hallowed to you. Here let your presence dwell and your glory be revealed. And grant that all who shall call upon you here may worship you in spirit and in truth, and may in their lives show forth your praise, through Jesus Christ, our Lord. Amen.

Dedication Benediction

MINISTER: Now unto him who is able to do exceeding abundantly above all that we ask or think according to the power that works in us, to him be glory in the church of Jesus Christ, throughout all ages, world without end. Amen.

Anthem

Readings: Joshua 24:15–24 "Renewing the Covenant" Matthew 7:24–29 "The Sure Foundation"

A Prayer for the Day

Offering and Offertory Response

Hymn: "Take Thou our Minds, Dear Lord"

Preaching of the Word

Prayer, Benediction, Amen

Recessional Hymn: "God of Grace and God of Glory"

Postlude

St. Paul's United Church of Christ
Summit Station, Pennsylvania
Gene W. Aulenbach, pastor

Dedication of Memorial Tree Plantings

MINISTER: To the Creator, our God and Father, who restores our souls and leads us to worship him,

PEOPLE: We dedicate these trees.

MINISTER: To Christ our Lord, who noted the beauty of all growing things, and who noted goodness in people and called us to grow to that goodness,

PEOPLE: We dedicate these trees, as a constant reminder of his creating and growing love.

MINISTER: To the Holy Spirit, who was first heard as the sound of wind moving through the trees of a garden,

PEOPLE: We dedicate these trees and we pray that as the wind moves through them in years to come, we may be reminded that we may also hear you, O God.

MINISTER: And so to you, Father, Savior, and Eternal Guide, we offer these trees,

PEOPLE: And we dedicate their growing strength as a symbol of our desire to grow, and may people in times to come find peace and shelter by walking among them.

MINISTER: To the memory of _____ we dedicate these evergreens as a symbol of everlasting life.

PEOPLE: Amen.

MINISTER: To the memory of _____ we dedicate this maple tree which loses its leaves each fall and becomes green again in spring, as a symbol of the resurrection of life that you grant to each of us.

PEOPLE: Amen.

Christian Union Church
Metamora, Illinois
Clifford J. Janssen, pastor

Consecration of Visitation Teams

MINISTER: Recognizing the sacredness of our common task, the congregation has invited you today in a simple act of consecration to be set apart for this service, dedicating time, talent, and substance, but first giving yourselves to him who gave himself for us all.

MINISTER AND VISITATION TEAMS IN UNISON: We give thee but thine own, whate'er the gifts may be. Our very selves are thine alone, a trust, O Lord, from thee.

MINISTER: What shall we render unto the Lord for all his benefits?

TEAMS: We will take the cup of salvation, and call upon the name of the Lord.

MINISTER: Jesus said, "If any one would come after me, let that person deny himself [herself] and take up his [her] cross and follow me." In presenting yourselves in this service you acknowledge the high calling of God in Christ Jesus.

TEAMS: And under his appointment and for his service we offer our time, our ransomed powers, our substance and ourselves, as he may guide us.

MINISTER: As you have been designated by the congregation for this service of enrollment, as its pastor under God, I commission you to perform this sacred service of enlisting us, our service and commitments, toward advancing Christ's kingdom through our local congregation.

TEAMS: Trusting him for wisdom and guidance, and our fellow Christians for the united and sympathetic support of his cause to which we also give ourselves, we accept the charge and go forth in service as unto him.

MINISTER: The Lord direct and greatly bless and use you to the honor of his name, the enlistment of his people, and the advancement of his kingdom. Amen.

Calvary Evangelical United Brethren Church
Cumberland, Maryland
Carl W. Hiser, pastor

Readings for the Dedication of Welcome-Card Pew Racks

"So then you are no longer strangers and sojourners, but you are fellow citizens with the saints and members of the household of God, built upon the foundation of the apostles and prophets, Christ Jesus himself being the chief cornerstone" (Eph. 2:19–20).

We at (insert name of congregation) are concerned that the stranger and the sojourner be welcome in our church and that these people feel to be, with all of us, fellow citizens and members of the household of God.

To this end, we try to greet those who are new among us every worship service.

The Board of Deacons and Deaconesses and the pastor seek to contact and visit, when possible, the newcomers in the name of the church.

The new card holders and welcome cards in our pews serve as a link in this chain of friendship between the stranger in our midst and (insert name of congregation.)

There is a sign over the door of another church which proclaims with welcoming words "Only a stranger once!" We hope this may truly be said of our church also.

Given in memory of _____ by _____, the meaning of the holders and cards of welcome in our pews is rooted in the past, in the love of home and family. The cards take their expression in the present as silent messengers of welcome to (insert name of congregation).

In their simple and yet truly significant way, may they serve to introduce many who are "strangers and sojourners" in our midst to our church for years to come.

Let us pray: Almighty God, help us ever to be a congregation concerned with the stranger. May there never be in our midst one who is lonely of heart and spirit who does not find the extended hand of friendship and the spoken word of welcome from us.

As we dedicate these welcome-card holders for our pews, we pray that you will bless them in the part they play in our congregation. May they serve as a link of love between our congregation and any who may sit among us as a stranger, that they may be a stranger only once. Hear us as we pray in the name of Jesus Christ, our Lord. Amen.

Summerdale Community Church
Chicago, Illinois
Kenneth Stokes, pastor